NEGOTIATING WITH PLANNING AUTHORITIES

A. Wenban-Smith MA, MSc, Dip TP, MRTPI
Managing Consultant, Segal Quince Wicksteed Ltd.

and

J. Beeston Dip TP, MRTPI
Birmingham Heartlands Ltd.

1990

Estates Gazette

THE ESTATES GAZETTE LIMITED
151 WARDOUR STREET, LONDON W1V 4BN

First published 1990
ISBN 0 7282 0148 8

*This book was commissioned
and produced for the Estates Gazette Limited
by Leaf Coppin Publishing Ltd*

Printed by Hobbs the Printers of Southampton

(431/90)

Negotiating with Planning Authorities

CONTENTS

FOREWORD

Sir Reginald Eyre

(Chairman of Birmingham Heartlands Ltd.,
Deputy Chairman of the New Towns Commission
and a former Parliamentary Under-Secretary of State
in Environment, Trade and Transport Departments)

I am delighted to have the opportunity to write a foreword to this book by Alan Wenban-Smith and Jim Beeston. I have often felt that many people in the landed professions do not have enough understanding of the processes and attitudes of government, at local or national levels. Such an understanding is a vital prerequisite to an important negotiation, for without it time can be wasted and opportunities missed.

In my view this book is an important contribution to enhancing the workings of the public and private sector to secure better developments, whatever definition one applies to the word 'better' in that context.

As chairman of a company which is dedicated to harnessing the skills and resources of both sectors to stimulate the regeneration of a large area of the inner city, I know only too well how difficult it is to overcome problems, and just how much negotiation, using the word in its widest sense, takes place.

I thoroughly recommend this book to all those involved in the property world. It adds to our knowledge and stimulates our thinking in a very practical way.

1 INTRODUCTION

Scope, Purpose and Standpoint

This book is about the negotiations with local planning authorities needed to achieve successful development. 'Success' is defined as mutual benefit to the developer and to the community that is host to the development. The assumption upon which discussion is based is that collaboration is more likely to be fruitful than conflict – and that even if conflict is inevitable, negotiation will limit it. This is important: successful developments need successful environments to support them, while local communities need regularly to attract investment from further afield in order to thrive. Neither side can afford to win too many total victories!

The negotiations with which the book is concerned will always have winning planning approval as their objective, but may require parallel agreements on questions such as access, infrastructure and land. These matters may also be within the power of the local authority.

This is not a handbook on negotiation, nor a text on planning law and procedures as such: these matters are part of the background. What the present work seeks to do, is to provide a guide to the complexities of local authorities' objectives, powers and limitations, and in so doing, to indicate what local planning authorities as well as developers should regard as good practice. Common understanding helps to avoid wasted effort and frustration on both sides, and thereby creates a better basis for a mutually beneficial relationship.

The scale and complexity of proposals vary enormously and few developments will raise all the issues covered here. The book is therefore designed for easy, selective reference.

A final caveat: in the complex and shifting pattern of legislation, market forces and social change, some of the finer details will inevitably change. This means that the practitioner will need to ensure up-to-date advice on such matters. However, the general principles outlined are relatively timeless, so long as mutual benefit remains an objective.

The Public Sector/Private Sector Relationship

To achieve mutual benefit through negotiation requires an appreciation of what constitutes a benefit to the other side, as well as one's own. Negotiations with local planning authorities are almost invariably across the public/ private sector divide and this creates a major obstacle to communication and understanding between the parties, and therefore to the conduct of negotiations. Developers often find local authorities slow to respond, indecisive and obsessed with procedures, and they speak as they find, attributing it to incompetence and/or ignorance. Local authorities, on the other hand, often find developers insensitive to the wider and longer term effects of their proposal, uncaring of the views of local people and obsessed with profit – in short, narrow-minded, callous and greedy.

This may be a caricature of the polarisation of public and private sector views, but, none the less, such attitudes – albeit unspoken – underlie many superficially civil encounters, and can prevent the best collaborative potential from being realised. Fundamental differences in roles and responsibilities lie behind the contrasting behaviours of public and private sector agencies, and the first step is to understand these.

Objectives

In the private sector these are relatively straightforward, concerning rates of return, capital growth and security/risk. Although the assessment of these factors in order to reach a decision may require skill, flair and technical sophistication, they are all definable in terms of a single aim – financial. This is in strict contrast to the public sector position where objectives may include economic growth and provision of jobs, which are directly related to the developer's assessments, but where concerns such as the character of the area, safety, traffic generation, noise, aesthetics, the implications for other parts of the town and the effect on future decisions must also be taken into account. These issues can be individually very complex and cannot, even in principle, be combined into a single criterion for decision analogous to a financial rate of return.

Accountability

The difference in the nature of the objectives is reflected in the decision-making processes. Public-sector decisions are ultimately about social values: how much local character, for example, should be sacrificed for how much economic growth? No amount of expertise (notwithstanding cost–benefit analysis) will provide a simple answer to such a question.

Society elects a set of people to make such judgements for it – and if those people offend too many members of the electorate too often, it elects another set. Developers often find this difficult to appreciate, because they are used to taking decisions on their own account, albeit having to persuade funding institutions to back them. Decision-making by elected members is different: not only do they have to attain complex objectives, but they are answerable to the electorate according to a legal framework requiring public bodies to be 'fair', and therefore consistent, in their treatment of those with whom they enter into business. This demands open processes of policy formulation, consultation and explanation. Rules, continuity, accountability and checks and balances mean paperwork and records; such bureaucracy takes time.

Mobility

The most important, most obvious, and most overlooked difference of all – a developer can walk away from an area, but the local authority can't!

Despite these difficulties there is common ground between public and private sectors in the mutual interest of developer and local authority in a successful development in a thriving community. The wider and longer term connotations of land and buildings, when compared with most other forms of investment, make practical approaches to the reconciliation of public and private interest in development particularly important.

The Current Context

If local authorities, as currently constituted, are no longer able to pursue distinctive local policies – whether in development or in other fields – as freely as in the past, this does not affect the general principle: the interrelationship of successful developments and successful places does not depend upon the form (or even the existence) of local authorities. But the alteration in status or position of local authorities does affect the detail. An awareness of the dynamics of change makes up part of the context of negotiation at any time.

In the field of planning, many changes have taken place quite independently of legislation: thinking in the planning profession has been moving away from the false certainties of rigid 'master plans' – plans which tried to take in advance most of the development decisions of the following ten years. The trend is towards a more continuous planning process, recognising the necessity for tactical flexibility and a degree of opportunism, but seeking to provide a coherent strategic framework in which investors and service providers can have some confidence. Such confidence is more likely to be inspired by a robust ability to adapt to change in a principled and purposeful way, than by the illusory certainty of colours on detailed maps (a good account of this shift is provided by 'Town & Country Planning', the report of a committee of inquiry appointed by the Nuffield Foundation, 1986).

These changes to the planning process have been paralleled by increasing understanding and awareness by planning authorities of commercial motivations – part of a wider movement towards greater overlap of public and private sector methods and perspectives. Local authorities no longer have the power – even if they had the desire – to dictate forms of development or the terms on which they would enter into partnerships to the extent that they did in the sixties and early seventies. While this period produced many adventurous and worthwhile additions and adaptations to outworn urban structures, it also produced numerous examples of both commercial shortsightedness and municipal *folie de grandeur*. The need is for a balance between the public interest and purely commercial considerations. Both sides have something distinctive to offer to the realisation of the aim of 'successful developments in successful places'. To achieve this is not easy: in addition to the intrinsic difficulties, there are people in entrenched ideological positions on both sides eager to seize upon failure. However, there are some promising examples of partnership and some of these will be used to illustrate practical points.

Whatever happens to local authorities, it seems likely that the emphasis on control through a regulatory (planning permission) process will continue to decline. The importance of other aspects of the overall negotiation will become more prominent – both to the local community as it seeks a return flow of benefits to the area, and to the developer as he seeks a supportive context and a stable, constructive future. Paradoxically, as the regulatory and financial powers of local authorities have been reduced, so their interest in more indirect means of achieving both development and resource objectives have increased: broadening the scope of negotiation is a means of increasing leverage. Looking beyond the development field, it is one of the ways in which local authorities are moving towards *enabling* the provision of services, rather than making direct provision themselves.

Yet, although systems can be transformed at the stroke of the legislator or administrator's pen, practices and people – and underlying economic, political and social reality – change more slowly, thus providing continuity to the context in which planning negotiations take place. As it is, different councils differ greatly in how entrepreneurial they are. The present book attempts to draw some general lessons from that variety.

Arrangement of Contents

The contents have been organised so that, for a particular type or style of project, the relevant sections can easily be consulted. Chapters 2, 3 and 4 consider the planning context within which any development proposal will be considered; other local authority functions that could be drawn into a wider negotiation and the planning and service issues that arise for the main different types of development. Chapters 5 and 6 examine the negotiation process itself, the former with the initial phases, and the latter with the forms of relationship that might evolve. In the case studies which are used in these chapters to illustrate practical points the factual details have been altered to prevent identification.

Development and the Planning System

A necessary condition for development of any kind is a planning permission. This chapter gives an outline of the planning system and its operation by different local authorities (LAs) in their role as local planning authority (LPA). For the simpler forms of development, this may be all the information required – along with that given in Chapter 4 on the principal use proposed.

For larger or more complex developments to be successful, planning permission may be only one of the matters for negotiation with the local authority. The point of entry in such cases is still likely to be the planning system, but it can then also be used to provide access to other appropriate departments and facilities (see further below, Chapter 5).

Since it is the local authority's 'front door' to the development world, the developer's understanding of the planning system and its requirements can be the key to other help which most planners would expect to provide. Conversely, the local authority is a political entity representing a local community, and may be less willing to enter into positive collaboration on other matters if its development policies are not respected.

Whether the development is large or small, the applicant needs to understand what the local planning authority is seeking to achieve through its planning policies, how far there may be a common interest and how far therefore the planning system and its legal framework may be a hindrance or a help.

The Planning System in Outline

The essentials of the planning system have remained remarkably unaltered since first comprehensively enacted in 1947: the requirements are for all development to have 'planning permission'; for local planning authorities to prepare 'development plans' and for 'regard' to be had to the development plan in determining whether planning permission should be given. Almost everything else is in continual flux: how much weight should be put on the development plan compared to other matters; what are legitimate concerns for the development plan; what should be the extent of 'blanket' permissions given by 'Development Orders'; what should be the balance between local and central policy-making, and so on. The current position is excellently summarised from a government standpoint in Planning Policy Guidance Note 1, DOE, January 1988.

Development Plans

The current system differs between the Metropolitan areas (Greater London, Greater Manchester, Merseyside, South Yorkshire, Tyne & Wear, West Midlands and West Yorkshire) and the rest of the country.

Non-Metropolitan areas Since 1968 the development plan for these areas has been in two parts: a 'structure plan', prepared by the county council, which deals with broad, long-term land use and transport policies for the whole county area and 'local plans' (generally prepared by district councils), which go into site-specific detail for particular smaller areas.

There is country-wide coverage of structure plans, but local plans have only been prepared for relatively few areas. Where there is no local plan, the detailed zoning of the pre-1968 county development plan remains in force, and may have some relevance (in particular it can affect the valuation of land for compulsory purchase (see below, p.44), and, in the absence of contrary policies in the structure plan, provides one of the starting points for what might be given planning permission).

The Secretary of State for the Environment has to approve a structure plan (and his Notice of Approval, which is usually a lengthy policy document itself, becomes part of the plan), while a local plan has only to be approved by the local authority that prepared it (after a public inquiry, if there are objections).

Metropolitan areas Until recently, the development planning system was the same as that described above. However, the GLC and the metropolitan county councils were abolished in April 1986, and their 'strategic' planning powers passed to the London boroughs and metropolitan districts. These are now therefore the custodians of the county-wide structure plans prepared pre-abolition. However, these structure plans will not be reviewed: a new planning system is being brought in whereby 'unitary development plans' (UDPs) are to be prepared by *each* metropolitan district and London borough for its own area. These combine the functions of structure and local plans in a single document, embracing both broad strategy and local detail. The UDP is generally to be approved by the LPA itself, though with reserve powers for the Secretary of State. The LPA must take account of any 'strategic guidance' given by the Secretary of State, and cannot begin the formal process of preparing a UDP until he has given a 'commencement order'. (The first of these were issued in February 1988, simultaneously with strategic guidance, to six West Midlands districts.)

In addition to the main forms of development plan, there are numerous types of plan performing a similar role for particular areas or purposes.

Enterprise zones   These have 'planning schemes' which are not dissimilar to local plans (and subject to a similar process of public inquiry) but go a step further in that they give planning permission for particular uses indicated in the scheme, subject to any conditions it specifies. Other uses can still be applied for in the normal manner, as can relaxations of conditions. Financial benefits are available for developers and occupiers.

Simplified planning zones   Simplified planning zones represent the extension of the enterprise zone planning scheme to other areas. Once again the key feature is that planning permission for a range of uses is given by the scheme. Provided this includes the desired use in the right location, and within an acceptable set of conditions, an application to the LPA for specific planning permission is not required.

Conservation areas   These do not zone land in the same way as the above, but do affect the kind of development for which planning permission is likely to be forthcoming, and also makes *demolition* subject to consent.

Informal plans   Informal plans, and other planning guidance of a non-statutory nature, may be prepared by an LPA to advise developers and others about its planning policies for an area (e.g. planning briefs or development frameworks) or type of use (e.g. planning policy statements).

The different strata of the planning system still extant in any given area, together with the various 'special purpose' types of plan (local and central), can lead to situations of some complexity.

Development Control

Is consent needed?   As noted above, development generally requires planning permission from the LPA. There are however numerous exceptions to the general need for specific planning permission:

There is a range of operations and changes of use which do not constitute 'development' for the purpose of the planning legislation: most are minor (like internal improvement and maintenance), but others can be major (like agriculture and forestry), and include a large number of changes within broad categories of activity, specified in the Town and Country Planning (Use Classes) Order – 'UCO' – 1987 (No. 764).

A further large range of developments is given 'blanket' permission by the General Development Order (GDO).[1] These are mostly minor, but some are significant (e.g. development on operational land by rail, gas, electricity and water undertakings, and extensions of 25 per cent or up to 1000m^2 on factories and warehouses). In addition, permission may be granted in advance by virtue of a simplified planning zone or enterprise zone scheme (see above), or by a special development order made by Parliament.

Procedure   The key points are:

application is to the district council in ''shire' areas, not to the county council;

anyone can apply (except on Crown Land), but they must notify the site owners (or long leaseholders);

the application can be in outline (to establish principle), or in detail;

the applicant must advertise and post a site notice for 'bad neighbour' proposals;

there is a special procedure where listed buildings are concerned;

the LPA is obliged to consult other bodies in certain cases, e.g. the highway authority (see below, p. 15) where there is a new access or material increase in traffic likely to a classified road; or the county where, in the opinion of the district, there is conflict with the structure plan;

if there is not a decision within eight weeks, the applicant is entitled to treat his application as refused, and to appeal;

there are application fees, roughly related to the scale of development;

the stages of the process that an application goes through are as follows (see also Appendix 1):

1. submission and receipt of application;
2. consultation (statutory, council-wide, general public);
3. formulation of officer's view and recommendation/report to committee;
4. committee decision and decision document (the planning permission).

Criteria for decision   The LPA must 'have regard to the provision of the Development Plan and any other material considerations',[2] and decide whether or not to grant permission, and, if so, whether to attach conditions.

1. Town and Country Planning GDO 1977 (SI No. 1977/289, as amended by SI Nos. 1980/1946, 1981/245, 1981/1569, 1983/1615, 1985/1011, 1985/1981, 1987/765).
2.. S. 29, Town and Country Planning Act 1971 (as amended): the wording has remained identical since 1947.

Although the legislation apparently gives LPAs much discretion in the exercise of planning powers, in practice this is limited by several factors.

There is appeal against the LPA decision to the Secretary of State (and ultimately to the courts on points of law). As a matter of policy, he operates a presumption in favour of development – it is therefore for a LPA refusing development to show that it 'would cause demonstrable harm to interests of acknowledged importance' (PPG1, para. 15) – and he threatens the award of costs against the LPA as a sanction.

The development plan's role is not decisive. It is *only* one of the material considerations which must be taken into account' (ibid. para. 13). This means the LPA cannot rely on conflict with its provisions as sufficient reason for refusal – each case must be 'decided on its merits'.

Both the Government and the courts have tended to restrict the 'other material considerations' to 'land use matters'; there is no clear definition of these matters, but narrower views have gained ground in recent years.

'Planning gain'   The issue of 'planning gain' touches on the central questions of the interaction of community and development. As a result perhaps of the unsatisfactory narrowness of ministerial and legal interpretations of planning law, developers and LPAs have found mutual advantage in agreements extending beyond the development, negotiated in parallel with a planning application. This avoids the problem that the scope for imposing positive obligations by conditions on a permission is very limited – yet without such obligations the permission could not have been granted. A common example is where the local road system is not of a high enough standard: the developer does not have the land or the powers to improve it, but is willing to pay the highway authority to do so. Planning gain is discussed in greater detail in Chapter 6.

Local Planning Authorities

Types of Planning Authority

In discussion of the planning system, three main types of planning authority were identified: the two-tier arrangement in the 'shire' counties, with the strategic planning role at county level and the processing of planning applications with the district; and the single-tier arrangement in London and the metropolitan areas, where districts are responsible for *all* planning functions (and all other local authority functions too).

In addition to these (and the long-established special case of joint planning boards for the Lake and Peak districts), a fourth type of planning authority has more recently been created: the urban development corporation. These have taken over the LPAs' development control powers for their designated areas. As a result of extensive land ownership at inception, and resources for land assembly and preparation, they do not need to rely much upon the development planning system to achieve their purposes. They tend rather to use non-statutory planning processes more akin to estate management and marketing plans (see further below, pp. 44-5).

Organisation

Most local authorities delegate their planning functions to a committee of elected members, who in turn often delegate the development control role to a sub-committee. There may be further delegation of simple, non-controversial cases to the chief planning officer – but legally power cannot be delegated to a single elected member, even though a chairman or council leader's view may in practice be the decisive one. The exact scheme of delegation will be specific to the authority, as will be the way in which functions are grouped. At member level, planning is often placed with transport functions; at officer level, combined departments, or looser associations ('directorates') generally combine a number of land and/or technical service functions together, e.g. planning and architecture; planning and economic development; planning and estates. There is huge variety, reflecting the particular priorities and ethos of each place.

The common factor, whatever the organisational arrangement, is the distinction between the functions of officers and those of elected members. The role of the member is to represent the community, to set the political objectives of the authority and to take the final decisions. The officers' role is to identify the issues that the authority needs to act upon, to provide technical advice on alternative courses of action and their consequences and to carry out the decisions of the authority. In practice, of course, individuals step outside these roles: officers are sometimes not politically neutral, members are not necessarily technically ignorant. In the process of debating a decision or a policy, while it is still in flux, there will usually be considerable overlap. This is both natural and healthy as long as the fundamental distinctions are not forgotten. Again, the nature of the relationship will be part of the local culture.

As far as a developer is concerned, the larger and more innovative or controversial a project is, *relative to the scale and nature of the place,* the more likely political involvement will be. Planning decisions are a matter of public interest, with full committee meetings open to all and copies of the report available.

Evolution of the Planning System

The most important point to make about the planning system is that *in practice* it now bears little resemblance to its original form. What was in 1947 a part of a comprehensively planned world is now an island in an unplanned 'ocean'. The underlying philosophy has changed beyond recognition: development plans have become an agenda for negotiation rather than a fixed programme, while local planning authorities have in many cases become positive parties to development rather than bodies simply resisting what they regard as undesirable change. This is only partly the result of national political changes towards a more market-oriented approach. It is also the result of planners learning that there is too much uncertainty in the real world for rigid blue-prints to work. There has, interestingly, been a convergence of view of both public and private sector thinkers towards a 'strategic' planning approach, in which a sense of direction informs decisions and choices at the tactical level, but no attempt is made to try to predetermine all of these.[1]

The current national balance between the three main planning activities – *plan making, development control* and *positive intervention* – means that planning manpower is split almost equally between these activities. Locally it varies enormously between authorities in ways that have more to do with social and economic history than with current political control.

The further north, and the larger the settlement, the more likely it is that the emphasis will be on promotion of development as opposed to its prevention. This is because the perceived need to replace worn out infrastructure and buildings is paramount, and takes precedence over other considerations – environmental and ideological. This does not mean that anything is acceptable: it does mean that there is a positive attitude to development, provided that there is sensitivity to local needs. In the south, and smaller places, high development pressures and innate resistance to change tend to produce a negative orientation. The less the development pressures, the more likely that the planning authority will be helpful!

All these points demonstrate the necessity for a developer to find out the characteristics of the relevant local planning authority if the relationship is to be one of understanding (not necessarily agreement).

1. An example of a flexible response to procedural requirements is Birmingham's 'delegated authority zone' process to help extensive phased renewal. An outline planning permission was given for the whole development and the planning authority delegated to the chief officer the responsibility for detailed approval of each phase. This provided the developer with the certainty he needed, together with a quick and flexible means for him to respond to changing circumstances; for the planning authority it retained reasonable control. Where the LPA is committed, this can be more efficient than a simplified planning zone (see p.8).

Penetrating the System

Departmental Structure

This section concentrates on the normal planning application process and on making contact with the right individual among those planners who handle applications in a process known as 'development control' (dc). In later sections the interrelationship between this section and other relevant departments is clarified.

For the purposes of development control, authorities are almost always divided up into geographic areas. These may relate to wards or constituencies; they may relate to geographic areas used to administer other functions of the council. Some authorities will have their development control staff dealing only with planning applications and related matters; others will have them as part of teams dealing with local plan making, or scheme implementation. However, most authorities are likely to have an 'area planning officer', who may well be the best entry point. Only for a development that were large relative to the size of the authority, or one which raised controversial or novel issues, would it be worth a developer making the initial approach to the chief planning officer or the chief executive. Reconnaissance – including informal contact with the area planning officer – should be the applicant's guide. If still in doubt, he should write to the chief planning officer for advice on whom to approach.

Although the area planning officer is the primary contact, there may be others within the planning department whose experience or skill may be applied to a particular case:

an application of strategic significance (i.e. a development affecting far more than its immediate environs) such as a large out-of-town shopping development may attract the attention of a strategic forward planner;

applications involving conservation areas or listed buildings may draw on an officer, perhaps an architect, experienced in dealing with historic buildings or areas;

an application, such as a town centre enhancement scheme, impinging on an investment programme of the local authority may involve the planner charged with implementing such proposals.

Planners, like architects, surveyors and accountants, all specialise. From the outset, having established contact, the developer must find out which specialists are concerned.

3 OTHER LOCAL AUTHORITY ROLES IN DEVELOPMENT

A local authority has a wide range of powers and functions other than operating the statutory planning system – and bringing these into play may be important for a successful development. To quote the final paragraph of the Government's Planning Policy Guide No. 1 on general policy and principles:

Positive planning

The planning system is only one, and by no means always the most important, of the instruments available to public authorities to secure improvements in the built and rural environments, and to protect those environments from the negative effects of economic and social change. Many local planning authorities are active in using the full range of powers at their disposal to improve the environment. Depending on their powers, authorities (including National Park authorities and urban development corporations) are engaged in land-use management, economic development, conservation, transport planning, traffic management, estate and property management, the development of tourism and leisure facilities, etc. While land-use planning and development control has limited capabilities, it can, when judiciously used in conjunction with other relevant powers, play an important part in helping to shape an improved and healthy environment in town and country.

Although the local authority role is currently in decline, there is no sign of an alternative system capable of operating on the same scale. While areas can be administered directly by Central Government (e.g. through urban development corporations), this has so far meant applying a lot of money to a small area over a short period of time. Most of the country will probably continue to have to rely on other methods.

Structures and Policy

Some of the local authority's powers and functions will be exercised through the same officer and member structures as the development plan and development control system – conservation, reclamation, and environmental improvement programmes are commonly handled in this way because of the direct linkages to land use planning. Economic development and development land assembly, preparation and disposal activities often originated in the planning function, and retain strong ties to it, even if now related to separate departments or committees. In addition, at the higher policy and political levels *all* the functions of the local council are seen as serving wider directions and purposes – whether or not this is expressed in a formal corporate plan or policy statement.

For a relatively small development any issues concerning other local authority functions would normally be identified during the consultation process, but large and/or complex proposals could mean bargaining between the different service committees. Such bargaining demands reference to some wider set of objectives, and a higher level of the power structure. This theme is returned to in later chapters, but for the present some of the most significant local authority functions which may become involved in a development negotiation are briefly described.

Types of Power

A distinction needs to be drawn between *statutory functions* and *discretionary abilities*. The first are *obligations* on a local authority, though it may have discretion on exactly how it carries them out (examples would be development control and provision of schools). The second category is much more varied, but there are two broad groups of activity: functions *enabled* by general (or local) acts (e.g. powers to purchase land for planning, highway or housing purposes); and the general power to spend a certain amount (at present the product of a 2p rate) on *any* purpose of general benefit to the area. In addition to these direct activities, the local authority is often an *agency* or access/delivery point for government and European programmes. Current examples include the Urban Programme, Derelict Land Grant and European Regional Development Fund grant. Although projects have to meet government criteria, there are usually many different ways of doing so. The local authority's stance can therefore be decisive – indeed, it is often the initiator. The principal roles of relevance are highways, landowner and financial enabler.

Highway Authority (in shire counties and metropolitan districts)

Except for trunk roads, the local authority as highway authority is responsible for building and maintaining all public roads in its area. It also has a wide range of powers to alter and to regulate the use of roads (including the right to veto planning applications which would lead to danger or to excessive interference with traffic flows); to buy land on which to build roads; to enter into agreements to carry out road works for a developer (for payment) and to take on the future maintenance of roads (e.g. estate roads in a housing area) dedicated to the highway authority.

Interestingly, there is no specific road or transport planning function allocated to the highway authority. Forward planning of transport systems generally is part of the development plan function described above (see p.7), under the Town and Country Planning Acts. This provides the basis for the identification of long-term road reservation lines, and of the principal road network, to which direct access may be restricted.

Short- and medium-term programmes of road improvement, plus a general synopsis of the local authority's transport policies, can be found in an annual document called the Transport Policy and Programme (TPP). Formally, this is a bid for money (transport supplementary grant) from a national pool for 'roads of more than local importance', and for authority to spend on roads generally (transport capital allocation), but many highway authorities use it also to explain their future intentions. However, programme dates in TPPs have to be treated with caution as they will be linked to the bid (which is invariably higher than the actual amount received), while priorities often change. Developers depending upon the prior construction of a road can influence programme dates – for instance, where substantial local benefit is seen to flow from a proposal, or where the developer meets part of the cost, thus improving the cost/benefit to the authority. These may be important negotiating points.

To take an example: an authority has back land which would be opened up by a road-widening scheme scheduled for ten years hence. There is no objection on planning policy grounds to a major retail development, but suitable access cannot be obtained without the road-widening scheme being carried out. Potential thus exists for a negotiated agreement under which the highway authority brings forward the road scheme in return for payment of a substantial part of its cost – part of the payment taking the form of land needed for the road.

Landowner

For historic reasons local authorities may be major land owners within their areas (and sometimes outside as well). The bulk of an authority's land holdings are likely to be tied up in the provision of particular services: school sites, housing estates, parks, playing fields. But the level and distribution of the need for such services are continually changing, providing some room for manoeuvre. In addition, there are left-over parcels of land following, for example, the construction of a road, while in central areas there are frequently extensive land interests, dating from comprehensive redevelopment schemes. There may too be specific endowments of land from former citizens, dedicated to the council for public use. Local authorities also have powers for compulsory purchase of land where this is necessary to the achievement of some public purpose.

Authorities vary greatly in how actively they make use of their land portfolio, from those that hoard land almost obsessively, through those that are simply unconscious of the scale or potential of their holdings, to those that operate in a manner barely distinguishable from a private sector developer. An increasing proportion would probably take (or could be persuaded to take) a view towards the active end of the range, i.e. that the purpose of a local authority holding land is to benefit the local community. Maximising that benefit is not simply a financial question, but implies a regular, critical review of whether particular pieces of land are in the most beneficial use, or whether the value of the land would not be better put to another purpose. Enlightened authorities are quite prepared to entertain ideas from others on these matters, the key point being that they will have non-commercial, as well as commercial, objectives. If the developer understands what these are, there is a far better chance of arriving at a mutually satisfactory conclusion.

The local authority's freedom of manoeuvre on land matters has changed since the heyday of development partnerships in the sixties and early seventies. It is now more common for a local authority's contribution to a partnership to be disposal of existing land interests rather than to be acquiring key sites through compulsory purchase order – but both modes of operating are still much in use. Whilst the Government has been pressing public bodies generally to dispose of surplus land, obstacles and disincentives have simultaneously been placed in the way of their actually doing so:

only a limited proportion of any amount realised can be used in each subsequent year to finance other capital spending;

capital spending as a whole is limited, and particular asset sales do not increase this limit;

even 'barter' deals (in which no money changes hands but a purchaser carries out works on behalf of an authority) can fall foul of the most recent restrictions – unless the Government is satisfied that the overall effect is not to leave the local authority with more land and property than it started with;

local authorities are required by law to obtain the 'best price' for disposals, unless they have the consent of the Secretary of State.

These are classic instances of the unintended side effects of one government policy frustrating the purpose of another. If this does not render co-operation on land ownership matters impossible, it does increase the determination that is required from both sides – and the ingenuity and sophistication needed to find mechanisms which produce satisfactory mutual benefit.

Financial Enabler

In a sense, the discussion above of the use of a council's land resources relates to the more general issue of the use of its financial resources, since the value in land could have been realised in cash terms. The word 'enabler' is used because in addition to the local authority's own financial interests, there is also its role in delivering other sources of finance – particularly the various grant regimes of Central Government.

In dealing with the involvement of an authority's own resources in development negotiations, it is necessary first of all to dispose of a surprisingly resilient myth: local authorities do *not* benefit financially from the increased rateable value arising from development. The main govern-ment grant to local authorities (currently the rate support grant) includes a complex financial levelling system, designed to put areas with high rateable values and low needs on a par with those having the opposite characteris-tics, in respect of their need to levy rates (or a community charge) locally. The side effect is that an increase in rateable value leads to an approxi-mately equal loss of grant.

This provides an interesting contrast with the USA, where not only do changes in the local taxable base directly benefit local authorities, but also they have a far wider range of ways of raising revenues – and these can be related closely to a particular public investment: e.g. a hotel bed tax to help pay for a tourist attraction. However, declining areas can easily be trapped in a vicious circle of increasing needs and decreasing tax base, raising tax rates and depressing services to the point that new private investment is driven away.

None the less, if *other* ways of supplying resources to the community can be found, then there is a wealth of examples to follow from the USA of successful public/private development partnerships. Imagination and so-phistication may be needed to achieve this in the context of the current web of financial regulations and controls.

The other form of direct financial involvement is when there are financial flows the other way. Many councils provide grants to encourage particular types of development, e.g. conservation grants for projects contributing to restoration of the heritage; or economic development incentives where a significant new source of employment or industrial investment would result. However, unlike a private company every payment by a local authority requires not only that there is the money in the bank (and that the payment is in accordance with the aims of the organisation), but also that there is a specific power, contained in an Act of Parliament, for the local authority to make the payment. This can present serious problems, particularly if the local authority has exhausted the resources available under the general power to spend up to a 2p rate product on projects of benefit to the area.

The other important class of financial involvement comes through local authorities' role as channel or guide for government and EEC funds. There is a vast – and ever-changing – kaleidoscope of these: some are directed at specific activities (e.g. DTI assistance to industry) but other regimes are specifically aimed at property development. A common feature is that local authorities are frequently a means of access to funds which might be particularly relevant to a scheme.

City grant   The city grant is the predominant source of grant funding for private sector inner city projects, and has absorbed the urban development grant, urban regeneration grant and the private sector derelict land grant. Central Government negotiates and pays the grant, but local authorities have to sanction applications as a planning authority and are encouraged to assist and support applications.

The city grant makes up the difference between the cost (including profit) and market value of a development project where projects have high costs (where ground conditions are poor, say) and/or where values are depressed. Schemes have to meet government criteria and value-for-money tests, and must contribute to urban regeneration. It is available only in specified urban areas, and for projects whose total value exceeds £200,000. It is entirely discretionary and subject to availability of funding (i.e. it is a competitive process).

Urban programme (UP)   Projects below that figure are eligible for urban programme funding if they are situated in areas where there is an urban programme. Similar criteria apply, but twenty-five per cent of funding comes from the local authority as is the case with all urban programme schemes.

Derelict land grant (DLG)   Private sector derelict land grant, funded at eighty per cent of the net loss of reclaiming derelict land, is now absorbed by the city grant. Public sector DLG is still available to local authorities, is a hundred per cent funding, and there is the opportunity, in carefully structured situations, for private land to pass through the local authority, benefit from the grant, and pass on again.

These grant regimes, together with conservation grants, are the most common forms of assistance to development projects, and the only forms generally available for speculative projects.

Occasionally there may be opportunity to approach other grant systems. The following is not an exhaustive list but highlights the most likely of the rarer opportunities.

1. European Coal and Steel Fund
   Public or private sector.
   Supports new economic activity in areas of coal and steel decline.
   Loan, often needs guarantee. Up to two per cent rebate of interest.
   Application to EEC via DTI or finance house.
2. Industrial Development Act (1982)
   Public or private sector (site owner).
   Site infrastructure to support industry.
   Applications to DOE or Department of Transport.
3. Sports Council
   Public or private sector sports projects.
   Relatively small amounts.
   Applications to Sports Councils (Regional).
4. Tourism
   Any developer who satisfies eligibility tests.
   15-20 per cent of capital cost.
   Strong criteria aimed at tourism strategies.
   Under £100,000, applications to Regional Tourist Board.
   Over £100,000, applications to National Tourist Board.
5. Rural Development
   Support to rural development projects.
   General small amounts.
   Applications to COSIRA (Council for Support of Industry in Rural Areas).

As a general rule grants to development projects have to satisfy the 'additionality' test, that is whether the project would happen in the agreed form *only* with grant aid. A high degree of understanding of the 'grantmanship' aspects of the various regimes is required. Without that, much time can be wasted on abortive applications. One critical aspect, though, is the support of the local authority, particularly where it plays the role of local motivator.

The Policy Agenda

As well as a variety of planning authorities, there is also a wide range of different policies that they may apply concerning land uses. However, while *policies* may differ, the *issues* that are the subject of those policies are fairly constant. The purpose of this chapter is to identify the main issues for three broad land use categories (housing, industry and commercial) since these headings will form part of the agenda of the negotiation between a developer and the LPA. The common ground that seems to exist as to the legitimate concerns and content of planning policies under these headings is also sketched in.

The scope and content of the planning system are not defined by the legislation – only the mechanics. This perhaps explains the system's ability to survive in national political environments quite different from the one in which it was set up. For instance, the legislation itself will not help either the LPA or the developer to find out by what specific *planning* criteria particular types of development should be judged. The original legislators would have pointed at the development plan for the area, and this should indeed still provide an answer to the LPA's policy agenda. However, issues may have arisen since the development plan was produced, and, moreover, the current official view is that the development plan is '*only one* of the material considerations which must be taken into account' when determining a planning application (PPG1, para. 13). So what are the others?

This is the soft centre of the British planning system – a source of much irritation (and consultants and lawyers' fees) on both sides. However, from a positive point of view what is not certain is a matter for negotiation. If it suffers from sloppiness and lack of certainty, the British system at least avoids some of the failings of undue rigidity which affect other planning systems. As to the further 'material considerations' to be taken into account, they are: government policy statements (circulars, etc.); case law (appeal decisions, high court judgments) and planning policy statements of local authorities. The contradictions that exist between (and often within) these sources provide a rich vein of ambiguity, to be mined by skilful negotiators!

Government policy about what constitute legitimate planning criteria is somewhat obscure. The prevailing legal opinion is that 'In principle ... any consideration which relates to the development or use of land is capable of being a planning consideration' (Cooke J in *Stringer v MHLG*, 1971), but the Government takes the view that such considerations must relate to the purpose of the planning system – 'to regulate development and use of land *in the public interest* [their italics]'. This public interest is not identified with the private interests of neighbours, or competitors – though it may include them. For example, the loss of an individual's view of open space would not on its own be a material factor, but where that open space was appreciated by many or contributed to local character, it could be that its loss was not in the public interest. Similarly, where individual shops would be affected by the trading impact of a shopping development, this would not be regarded as a material factor, but if there were an impact on a whole shopping centre then there would be a question of the public interest. Thus the planning merits of each particular case would seem to depend on reference to some wider view of the public interest in land use matters, including (but not restricted to) those set out in the development plan. Some guidance is provided by circulars, and by Development Control Policy Notes (now being superseded by Planning Policy Guidance), but these tend to be more concerned with the question of what policy should be *about* rather than what it *is*.

Case law arises mainly from planning appeal decisions, increasingly decided by the planning inspectorate: they have to bridge the gap between the lofty generalities of circulars and the knotty local issues, using 'reasonable man' rules of thumb and precedents. Those cases recovered (or, in rare cases, called in) for the Secretary of State's own decision tend to be highly particular and political, yielding little in the way of policy direction applicable to other cases. The result is a system approximating to common law in its reliance on precedent, but lacking in accepted fundamental principles to which appeal can be made – an unhappy compromise.

Local authorities try to plug the gap: in addition to the development plan, most LPAs have a wide range of statements about particular policy areas (e.g. retailing), or about particular sites (planning briefs), or about their general approach to site-specific matters of detail (e.g. design guides). The status of these on appeal tends to depend on whether they have the benefit of a degree of local consensus, following consultation; and whether or not they are in conflict with national guidance.

These sources may all be reduced to two kinds of planning criteria: those relating to *policy*, and those that are *site-specific*. The issues under each of these will tend to be much the same anywhere; the particular local stand taken by the LPA will vary according to the needs, circumstances, history and politics of the place. Below is some guidance on what the issues are, and how (and within what limits) they will vary from place to place. But this can only be a start: for the developer, one of the first objectives of meeting with the LPA must be to establish clearly the local agenda for the particular development in question.

Housing

Housing is by far the largest single development use of land (about fifty per cent of the total), and consequent uses (open space, schools) account for most of the rest.

Policy issues on the agenda for housing developments of any size follow from this: location relative to planned provision; land supply; environmental effects (especially countryside, agriculture and green belt); scale/timing relative to infrastructure and service provision. The last two of these spill over into the site-specific: the issues of design in relation to the general character of the area, and access.

Location

Government-approved county structure plans exist for the whole country, and these specify amounts of housing land to be identified (either by allocation in local plans, or by granting of planning permission), over the plan period. This is usually broken down between administrative districts, often with specific amounts assigned to major named locations. Local plans will identify specific sites for some of the total amount; but some – perhaps even most – will be up to prospective developers to find. The first question for any significant scale of development (more than, say, ten units) will be whether or not it accords with development plan provision.

Land Supply

The amounts proposed in development plans are not sacrosanct. Arguments can be mounted for more (or less) to be made available because of 'other material considerations': for example, changes since the development plan was drawn up in household formation rates, net movement of people in or out of the area, or rates of clearance of older housing. Local authorities are supposed to ensure that five years' supply at the structure plan rate is specifically identified (of which two years' worth is immediately available). In most parts of the country, regular studies are published comparing the identified supply with that required, and commenting upon the results. This information is of great relevance to both LPAs and housing developers. It affects the relative strength of their negotiating positions because, although a deficiency or surplus is not decisive, the Government has said that it will be taken into account in deciding appeals (PPG3, para. 26).

Although there is a substantial quantity of government advice on the conduct and use of Housing Land Studies, they are essentially negotiated statements between local authorities and local representatives of the building industry (usually under the umbrella of the House Builders' Federation), and interpretations vary (even those of the DOE's regional offices); it is worthwhile for a developer to check the local position.

Environmental Policy

Most environmental issues will, by their very nature, be site-specific – but at the broad policy level there may be green belt, countryside and agricultural questions where land is being developed for the first time. While green belt policy is clear (and almost invariably supported on appeal), countryside and agricultural policy are shifting under the combined weight of agricultural surpluses and development pressure for housing (especially in the more economically successful regions). LPAs will usually be under strong local political pressure to protect the character of non-green belt countryside, if somewhat hamstrung by the absence of planning control over agricultural operations. Government support for this (except in Areas of Outstanding Natural Beauty) has been extremely patchy, since its free market intellectual stance is frequently in conflict with its supporters' emotions. County authorities will tend to have a more detached view about where development should go than districts, because counties have to make overall plans work.

In urban areas, the environmental emphasis at the policy level may be less to do with the effect of the development on the rest of the area than vice-versa: are noise, pollution or hazard levels acceptable for future occupants of the houses? These kinds of issues may require a widening of negotiations between developer and LPA to consider abatement measures, reclamation or protection/removal. A closer parallel to the rural situation is provided by the development of open space or playing fields: the LPA may have standards for provision at a neighbourhood level, but it might be possible for a developer to negotiate development of part of a site in return for enabling a more intensive or more widely available use of the rest. Density of development may be a policy issue – requirements may be minima (e.g. for high densities) to make use of limited land or expensive infrastructure or maxima (e.g. to protect from over-development).

The following example indicates the kind of planning negotiation that can take place between a developer wanting to provide housing and a local authority.

Case Study

An application by a church, in an industrial area, to develop an old persons' housing scheme next to the church, together with a day-care centre and other support facilities.

Despite support for the principle, the application was refused largely on the grounds that introducing housing especially for old people would inhibit the operation of neighbouring factories.

The local authority found a site suitable for the complete scheme, involving a new church, and made it available at a reasonable price. Extra housing for rent was also introduced and an urban development grant was provided for that housing. Funding from various sources was skilfully meshed together by the Church and their advisers.

Result: total success.

Environment and Design at Site Level

Where a small amount of development relative to that already existing is proposed, an important bench-mark is likely to be the 'established character of the area'. This may be taken as the amalgam of density, height, design, price bracket: the further the developer wants to depart from these, the stronger the case he must mount. The implication is that the public interest includes an element of predictability in the nature of further development that may take place (however, Secretaries of State have made plain their view that this does not amount to a cost-free restrictive covenant). The character of an area can be changed (and indeed changes gradually anyway), but there is an understandable resistance to change that affects people's living conditions and property values, and this is reflected by the decisions that elected members take. Correspondingly, the developer wishing to bring about change may have to make concessions or offer other benefits. These may be in the form of, say, landscaping or retention of trees or hedgerows, such as might form the subject of conditions, or may be more substantial forms of planning gain (see next section and chapter 5).

For larger developments, which effectively create their own environment, the existing character of the area may be a less significant constraint (though rarely negligible). Areas where there is a high level of development activity may wish to create identifiable characteristics on a larger scale in order to evolve a sense of place. Usually this is done through advisory measures, such as design guides and supplementary planning guidance in local plans. There may be mutual benefit in such measures: certainly they form part of planning negotiations.

Services and Infrastructure

There are two types of services involved in the case of housing: those required for the development to go ahead (e.g. roads, sewers), and those required as a result of the housing being occupied (e.g. schools, clinics, shops). With smaller developments, only the first is likely to have a bearing on planning permission: it is difficult to prove, for instance, that a critical threshold for school places will be breached by any particular small development even though a succession of such developments could well have this effect. Utilities such as water, gas and electricity must normally be requisitioned by the developer from the appropriate agency and they may well require payments to extend their networks to remote areas, or to increase thresholds, but these are not the specific concern of the LPA (the *generality* of infrastructure provision is discussed between LPAs and service agencies during the plan-making process). However, roads and schools are the concern of the LPA, as they are partly financed from local taxation, which it must raise; other services, such as shops, may not be the local authority's responsibility to provide, but could have a bearing on the planning of the area.

The government view (PPG3, para. 32) is that the relevant issue is the scale and duration of any harm arising from proceeding; and it encourages the use of planning gain agreements to secure necessary improvements. Larger scale developments could throw up a range of such considerations, especially where existing infrastructure is already stretched. Further matters then arise, such as whether spare capacity created by a new road, for example, should be allocated to the first developer, or rationed so as to last for a time. There may well be different answers in different places to this kind of question. It is certainly an area with potential for negotiated settlements.

Industry

Industry is a much smaller scale land user than housing – typically five to ten percent of urban development. Moreover, a wider range of industrial uses is either permitted development under the General Development Order, or not development at all (under the Use Classes Order). Nevertheless, most LPAs are anxious to attract new industry to their areas and there are significant matters that can crop up on the planning agenda. Policy matters may include implications for employment generation; scarcity factors affecting the value for the use proposed relative to other needs of the local economy and the mixture of uses proposed. Site-specific matters will include environmental effects, safety and access.

Employment

In most parts of the country, the employment generated is an unequivocal advantage, but in some of the most highly pressured areas of the south east, the reverse is the case. In both cases, this is because industrial uses – even those that do not directly employ large numbers of people – sell most of their output beyond the local area, and therefore generate economic growth. This in turn attracts further business and personal services, and additional population. Where countryside, existing housing and services are under pressure, this is less welcome than in areas where there is high unemployment and spare capacity. In these latter areas, there may well be pressure for the highest possible density of employment on the site, even though the overall employment effect in the local economy may only be very loosely related to this.

Scarcity Factors

Industrial requirements are not uniform; particularly for larger scale products and processes, site requirements can be quite severe. Those LPAs that are anxious to attract industry often therefore provide for a range of different types and qualities of location, so that no worthwhile project is lost for want of a suitable site. Inevitably, the demand for small-scale sites is much steadier than that for large-scale ones with particular attributes, while the environmental and access factors that make a site attractive for a large-scale development also make it so for a succession of smaller ones. Generally, the risks of relying on the planning system to safeguard scarce and valuable locations from piecemeal use are such that LPAs with such concerns will seek landlord control through purchase.

Mixture of Uses

LPAs tend to resist the use of industrially zoned land for commercial purposes, partly because of the need to maintain an adequate supply of good quality land for industrial investment, partly because of potential incompatibilities between users and partly because of fears of undermining existing commercial centres. However, they recognise that many industrial uses – particularly at the high technology end of the market – have substantial office or office-type content, which needs to be in close association with the manufacturing elements. It is these requirements that led to the combination of office and light industry uses into one class (B1 of the 1987 Use Classes Order).

A possible negotiating point here for the developer is to propose in return for an element of commercial use to bring forward the provision of infrastructure thereby making the rest of an industrial location more readily available for industrial use.

Environment and Safety

It is the job of the Health and Safety Executive to ensure that safeguards about dangerous materials, processes and emissions are observed. However, there are many aspects of industrial development that fall outside its concerns, but which nevertheless are of concern to LPAs. Noise, smoke, smells, traffic generation and visual intrusion will all be factors in the judgement as to whether an industrial use should be located in a particular area. Some uses are inherently 'bad neighbours', and require special locations away from housing or other sensitive areas. But in many other cases, layout, buildings, landscaping and accesses can be designed in such a way as to keep impact within acceptable limits. Much depends on the willingness of developers and planners to negotiate imaginatively, and to present the LPA with a package of conditions and legal agreements that is seen to address the issues and to be enforceable in practice.

Infrastructure and Services

The points made above concerning housing (see p. 27) also apply here.

Commercial

Commercial uses, principally shopping and offices, account for only a tiny fraction of developed land (around two to three percent). Existing concentrations of commercial uses tend to be in city, town or district centres, where there are advantages of propinquity and accessibility to both customers and other businesses. However, they generate land values which are typically ten times those of industrial or residential uses, and there is therefore strong pressure from developers for such uses in new locations, if there is a prospect of viability. In addition to land values, there are other forces favouring decentralisation, the most important of these being the declining accessibility by car of main centres relative to other locations. This is an unstable situation, with major implications not only for the centres themselves, but also for our settlement patterns and ways of life. With this backdrop, it is hardly surprising that the siting of commercial uses is the most intensive area of conflict between LPAs and developers.

At the level of the individual project, this means that the policy considerations will revolve around impact, that is, the effect on the viability of other existing or proposed developments. The most common site-specific agenda items relate to design, access and parking.

Impact

In retailing, marginal advantages of location translate into major changes in market share, making it the most volatile commercial use. Office uses are not so unpredictable, but in traditional centres there is a symbiotic relationship between the two (shared infrastructure, services, townscape and often buildings). LPA concern about impact will principally relate to retail proposals. The essential policy issue is whether the effect of such a proposal (taken together with other recent or concurrent changes) will seriously affect the vitality and viability of an existing centre *as a whole*. Scale, location, nature of goods sold and style of trading all affect this issue and represent potential points for negotiation between the LPA and the developer. On a grander scale, linked development or improvements to maintain the competitiveness of the original centre could be considered. A consequence of the threat of new commercial centres is a generally welcoming stance from LPAs for development that reinforces an existing centre.

Design

Commercial development is intensive and in very public locations: its design will therefore be a matter of great interest to the LPA as well as to the developer. Their opinions may differ on design for reasons other than taste: the LPA has to consider the broader questions of future development potential, townscape, conservation, pedestrian access and flows, microclimates and local servicing, all of which require the design of an individual building to be constrained by that of the existing or prospective neighbouring buildings. There may also be a desire on the part of the LPA to differentiate its particular main centres from the national generality. This can be helpful to the developer too, since such differentiation can be an important marketing point. Most of the negotiating advantages on design, other than a limited power of delay, are in the hands of the developer, except in the special cases of listed buildings and conservation areas. However, commercial development is an issue where mutual benefit should particularly be the touchstone: the quality of design of a centre is a selling point for all who do business there. Forcing through an unsympathetic design for short-term financial reasons will backfire on the perpetrator if the longer term attractiveness of the area to people, and hence customers and tenants, is thereby undermined.

Access and Parking

The intensiveness of commercial uses means that access requirements may be heavier than for other uses. Most planning authorities require developers to provide parking space adequate for the demand that their development will generate, and will usually have a set of norms relating this to the floor space and use. In some locations this may be physically impossible or extremely expensive, but there may be an opportunity for the developer to make a contribution to public car-parking provision in the vicinity through a planning gain agreement. Very often the standards of parking provision suggested by the letting agent will be higher than those requested by the LPA.

Purpose and Conduct of Negotiation

The aim of negotiation is to identify and draw together the differing perceptions of the parties in order to agree a final outcome: in this case a development project. The progress of negotiation will tend to fall into three phases: reconnaissance/briefing (to identify issues); the substantive stage (resolving the issues) and tidying up (formalising the agreement). Throughout the discussions normal negotiating techniques will generally bear fruit. This is not a handbook of such techniques – but some basic points need stating for completeness.

Both sides need to be briefed before a meeting. They need to try to predict the issues which will be raised, and determine how they will respond.

The developer needs to consider the tactics to be used. These can include inducements (see below, Chapter 6, on planning gain), threats ('I will build my factory somewhere else'), persuasion, activation of commitment and so on.

Both sides should ensure that there is mutual understanding and interpretation of the position reached.

Both sides must check that implementation matches both the spirit and the letter of the agreements to ensure satisfactory progress.

The Phases of Negotiation

Reconnaissance/Briefing

'Time spent on reconnaissance is seldom wasted,' Napoleon said. The purpose of this stage is for the developer to define the agenda, identify the issues and establish the process. In particular, the applicant's reconnaissance, by means of desk research, local contacts and/or initial exploratory meetings with the LPA, should cover:

The political complexion of the council   This means finding out not simply which party is in power, but where the balance of power sits within the spectrum of each party. (The common belief is that left-wing tory and right-wing socialist councils are more likely to be sympathetic to property development interests) See also Chapters 2 and 3 on penetrating the system and on the structure and policies of local planning authorities.

The personalities   The developer is advised to discover the relative position or strength of the personalities involved − officers, chairmen of committees, ward councillors or MPs, amenity societies and residents' groups, as far as is likely to be relevant to the project. The interplay of personalities may have a crucial bearing on the progress of a planning decision. The planner's role is to advise on ways and means, put issues on political agendas and implement decisions. Although the planners will sometimes be overruled by the politicians, they will all have worked together over time, and there can be a high degree of mutual understanding: they are, in a sense, in a continuous process of negotiation.

The motivation of the council   What is thought to bring most votes? Is it jobs and economic activity? Is it housing for local people? Is it defending the green belt and stopping urban sprawl? Is it ensuring the competitiveness of the place is boosted against (perceived) threats from others? There is a tendency for the answers to these questions to depend on geographical factors: to the north greater emphasis is placed on promotion as against control. However, there are variations, and it is part of the developer's task of reconnaissance to find out what these are.

These considerations are what can be termed quasi-political issues, where the local balance will depend on local circumstances. It is vital to recognise that, though local, these issues are very real and should not be dismissed by the developer. They are just as important as the more technical factors, to which we now turn:

The site and the scheme   The developer should never get himself into the position of an agent who confessed, following three meetings with a local authority to discuss a residential layout, that he had not actually visited the site.

Local practice and procedure   The developer needs to know the relevant legislative background and how this works. He or she should not, for instance, come away from a preliminary meeting without knowing who is actually taking the decision on the planning application − officers under delegated powers, a sub-committee, full committee or the council itself. How often does the relevant body meet? What is the lead time? Is this application likely to be called in by the Secretary of State? These are the sort of practical questions which the developer should be asking.

The overall planning context   This is an important and complex issue (see also Chapter 2 above). In addition to explicit policies, there may also be hidden ones, often evolving out of the grind of regular decision making ('policy making on the hoof'). Thus, a proposal for housing might be examined in the light of policies, both stated and hidden, as follows:

Government circular	Five-year supply of housing land to be maintained
Structure plan policy	2000 houses to be provided within the borough by 1991
Local plan	Defined sites to be developed or not, e.g. no development east of the by-pass
Informal plan	Design guide dealing with advice on house design, estate layout, etc.
'Policy on the hoof'	E.g. 'we do not like mock-Georgian houses in this location any longer'

Such preparation should ensure the developer is fully briefed and aware of the issues likely to be raised.

The Substantive Phase

Style and approach   All local authorities, for reasons of public accountability, have strict codes of conduct, which govern the relationships between officers and members and the people they deal with on behalf of the authority. If the resultant attitude may appear petty or narrow-minded, it should be borne in mind that some commercial approaches can conflict with public service codes. A helicopter flight over the site followed by lunch is not the sort of invitation the local authority officer can accept. Equally, although local authorities may be used to being threatened, elected members, in particular, do not like being backed into a corner. The 'unless I get planning permission within a week for my blood boiling factory in the green belt I shall take my investment elsewhere' approach has little chance of success. As in all negotiations the developer should define a series of fall-back positions and extra pressure points, while always giving the other negotiator room for manoeuvre. The developer also needs to remember he is dealing with individuals and must learn to distinguish between personal preferences and council policy.

Two key factors of style and approach pervade the whole process of negotiation: negotiating at the right level in the hierarchy and not over-lobbying which can be counter-productive. Chief Officers do not like being bothered by pre-submission discussions on chicken coops. It offends their status. (Moreover it makes them suspicious: is this chicken coop a front for a factory farm?) Conversely, the developer should not call on spec at the enquiry counter to discuss a million square foot shopping scheme. The approach should be at the right level and manner for the scale of the project, preferably with notice of issues so that the appropriate people can be gathered together for a meeting. As stated above, the area planning officer is a good place for the applicant to start. Even better, a clear letter from the developer in advance, addressed to the chief planning officer, gives him the chance to decide who is to be initially responsible.

Local authorities are encouraged by government circular to set out all the issues confronting a planning application at the earliest stage and not to raise fresh issues following successful resolution of these problems. These should be managed by means of a summing-up process, the aim of which is to leave a meeting with both parties clearly in agreement as to what has been agreed or otherwise, and what either party has then to do in order to advance. At this stage over-lobbying can raise barriers or create delay. For instance, a letter sent to an MP may be forwarded to the relevant civil servant in a 'red-jacket'; this will effectively stop all work on the project while the letter is answered. Probably the best approach is for developer and LPA to agree dates for specific pieces of action at their meeting: if these are not held to, then some follow-up is both legitimate and necessary.

Keeping in touch   Once the initial contact has been established, there are good reasons for the developer to stay in touch with the local authority during the whole process of formulating the proposals: it helps to generate involvement and commitment to success, and avoids unpleasant surprises for both sides. However, the following stages in the process are critical and demand more attention:

1. When the *proposals are formulated in outline* but not finally developed, a meeting will be an integral part of briefing the developer for future negotiations and will establish the LPA's initial view on the merits of the proposal.
2. As the *detailed proposals* emerge – immediately prior to submission – it is valuable for the developer to gain a more detailed, yet still informal, view from the planners, and also to establish the procedure they will use in dealing with the application, i.e. whom they will consult, possible references to DOE, etc.

3. At the point that the consultation process has been concluded and the planner is *formulating his recommendation* to the committee, negotiation by the developer can sometimes resolve or ameliorate objections to the scheme and concentrate the mind of the planner on the positive aspects affecting his recommendation.

4. *Following an adverse decision* (refusal, deferral, or unacceptable condition), the developer should always seek to establish whether the decision is made by the elected members against the recommendation of the officers. The developer should already have established the nature of the officers' recommendation.

5. If *an approved scheme* has to be amended by the developer in order to satisfy third party funders, to make the scheme viable or to satisfy a market opportunity, the local authority may be unhappy. Planning authorities sometimes feel that good (expensive) schemes are submitted to gain an approval, only for subsequent negotiations to reduce the scheme to (affordable) mediocrity. The developer should be as open as possible about the reasons for change.

It is important for the developer who is negotiating with a planning authority to make proposals and counter proposals; to read the feedback at all times; to test alternatives and to bring new forces to bear, or widen the case or issues.

Tidying up

It is vital to ensure that what has been agreed is properly reflected in the documents produced at the end of the process. If an approval is being recommended, the developer must pay particular attention to conditions which are to be attached to the approval. It will be far harder to have them changed after committee approval. Similarly, the developer must pay particular attention to the wording of any legal agreements: do they reflect his understanding of the agreements reached?

Negotiations introducing other Local Authority Functions

Despite the drift towards greater central government control and influence, local authorities are still uniquely placed to respond to development projects in a whole range of ways, in addition to their planning functions. Chapter 3 discussed the roles of highway authority, landowner and financial enabler. These can be put together in various ways:

1. As local planning authority acting with the local highway authority in a statutory fashion.
2. As a land owner acting in a commercial manner within the council's planning policy parameters.
3. As a promoter of development within their area, by their own development schemes, by direct grant aid, or by introducing schemes to other grant regimes.
4. As a publicist for their area.

The sum of these parts adds up to rather more. For example, the planning process results in the collection and analysis of extensive information: continuous involvement in the development process ensures the local authority has a full record of the local processes of change, from a strategic over-view to detailed knowledge of projects in the pipeline. Although this will not necessarily be set out from a developer's point of view it can be used by him to uncover information about competing projects, future infrastructure and schemes reinforcing the area's attractiveness. Such knowledge may be significant in securing funding for projects. It can certainly enhance a prospectus aimed at potential funders.

However, there are material differences between the role of the council as LPA and its role in these other functions, and they may well affect negotiations. While the approach to planning control is likely to be similar from authority to authority because of the statutory framework which defines not only the process but also its administration, authorities can act more individually in so far as land, economic development, promotion and publicity are concerned. Thus, each authority will have a different management structure, a different approach to the private sector, and a different way of promoting its area. The local balance depends upon local circumstances, with, as previously discussed, high development pressures leading to a more negative orientation on the authority's part. The north/south divide and urban/rural differences in this respect are apparent to most investors and developers.

Negotiating with Officers

A straightforward planning issue will be negotiated with a planning officer. But as cases become more complex, a whole range of officers may be concerned, both specialists from within the planning department, and others from different departments with a special role to play – environmental pollution or highways, say. Should the application encompass council-owned land, or financial support, then the net will be drawn wider still. Generally, the larger the authority, the more specialisation there will be. Smaller authorities may well be easier to deal with administratively – though they may lack the relevant expertise.

However, if public sector bureaucracies are fairly similar to private sector bureaucracies in terms of structure, they are very different when it comes to aim and purpose. A local authority has no single aim correlating to that of profit in the private sector, but rather several, often conflicting, objectives. Typically there is tension between the 'policeman' roles of the local authority, and the 'promotional' role. The resolution of such conflicts is often confusing to the outsider – indeed the very appearance of conflict in the first place may be difficult to comprehend. In many cases, it will be the planning process which resolves the conflicts – but not always. The manner of the resolution may depend upon the relative power of the various members or officers within the authority; this may in turn depend on the prevailing attitudes of the authority. Open conflicts are more likely to emerge in authorities which are firmly in the control of one party – and likely to remain so for the foreseeable future. Where political control is more finely balanced, conflicts are usually determined by informal means, by an *ad hoc* meeting of chairmen or senior officers, for example.

Ultimately, if the conflict arises from a planning application then it is the planner who has to make a recommendation to the politicians, and it should be a recommendation based on planning principles and not on matters which are *ultra vires*, i.e. outside the framework of planning law. In general, if other legislation exists to effect a remedy to a potential problem, then that legislation should be used and not the planning acts.

A Case Study

> *The site*   There is an empty factory in a rundown industrial area, close to a churchyard and open space. Planning policy is to encourage housing around the churchyard, but to retain industrial zoning of site.

> *The proposal*   To redevelop for housing purposes. Following negotiation, planners agree that residential zoning can be stretched to include site, as part of a wider policy of encouraging residential use back into the area.

> *The issue*   A planning application for housing is submitted. The environmental health officer objects on grounds of disturbance from nearby factory which causes vibration and noise.

The solution   The environmental health officer withdraws his objection if a condition is imposed on the planning approval to provide for insulation and a means of ameliorating the vibration. The developer accepts this condition to make progress.

The next issue   The developer undertakes technical studies using specialist consultants and discovers that the cost of providing the remedies effectively makes the scheme unviable. There is some doubt as to whether a full remedy as required by the planning condition can be technically satisfactory. A compromise is achieved.

There are a number of points which the case study illustrates:

1. The importance of proper professional advice at the right time. Most planning negotiations can be quite satisfactorily handled by one agent. But just as complicated development projects need extra specialist skills, so may complicated planning submissions.
2. A quick planning decision encumbered by all sorts of conditions is not necessarily the best approach. It may be preferable to take an extra week or two to resolve the issues properly: a quick planning approval can sometimes mean a slower overall process (the government practice of assessing planning authorities' performance in terms of percentage of applications determined within the statutory period can encourage bad decisions, though this is not a general excuse for slow planning decisions).

There can be no hard and fast rules for an applicant faced by conflicting views within an authority. Those close to the negotiation have to use their own judgement. Options open to the struggling applicant include: continuing to negotiate with the relevant officers; seeking discussions with a more senior or chief officer or lobbying committee members or the chairman. Actions not recommended to developers are writing to Central Government (other than a formal appeal), lobbying figureheads (e.g. the Mayor or Lord Mayor), or lobbying MPs who, it should be remembered, have no direct mandate within a local authority.

6 DEVELOPING PARTNERSHIPS

Towards Partnership

Local authorities are creatures of the law, and they can only act in ways for which there is a specific power granted by an Act of Parliament. Since the various elements of local authority activity are defined by separate Acts of Parliament, different objectives have priority according to the section of the local authority in question. A great deal of skill and compromise is necessary on the part of local authorities to achieve a single rational objective. None the less, there are some general powers, and the more enterprising authorities use their wit to make the most of the discretion that exists, and to act corporately in bringing to bear the whole range of specific powers.

However, over the last ten years the Government has acted consistently to exercise more control of local authorities. The stated purpose of this is to regulate public spending, but one side effect is to make it more difficult for local authorities to play a positive role in partnership with the private sector, in creating attractive and successful towns and communities.

There is a spectrum of possible relationships between local authorities and developers. At one end is the 'pure' planning approval relationship described in the first part of Chapter 5. This develops into arrangements including planning gain and development agreements which in turn culminate in partnerships that can involve a local authority's land ownership and joint venture agreements. While the planning process is tightly constrained by law, circulars and court decisions, further along the spectrum, activities are rather more akin to normal commercial transactions. The planning part of such an agreement must stand on its own feet, and be publicly defensible as a planning decision, and similarly there must be accountable legal form given to the other aspects – but how the parties reach that goal is not directed by law.

Partnership based on Planning

Planning Conditions

The relationship that results from planning negotiations will depend upon the conditions to a planning approval. General advice on the content of conditions is set out in Circular 1/85 (see Appendix 3 for a select list of government circulars). LPAs are advised to impose conditions only when they are:

necessary (without them consent would have to be refused)
relevant to planning (and not seeking to enforce matters controllable by other legislation)
relevant to the development permitted (and not seeking to deal with matters outside the purview of the application)
enforceable (e.g. not requiring full supervision)
precise
reasonable in all other respects

If a condition is not justified by the test of necessity then it needs special and precise justification (in other words, DOE is saying, there is an almost certain chance of success on appeal against such a condition!). Conditions can, incidentally, set up a continuing, albeit ultimately limited, relationship, e.g. where approval of further details is required, of where reinstatement of land or maintenance of landscaping is stipulated.

Planning Gain

The next possibility along the spectrum is an agreement between developer and LPA on matters which cannot be legally secured or enforced by the use of conditions attached to a planning permission. These are generally positive obligations, hence the term 'planning gain'. The legal mechanics available are described in more detail in Appendix 2. Briefly they are:

Section 52 of the Town and Country Planning Act 1971   This enables local authorities to enter into agreements with persons having an interest in land for the purpose of *restricting or regulating the use or development of land*. Negative covenants can be enforced against successors in title.

Section 33 of the Local Government (Miscellaneous Provisions) Act 1982
Positive obligations can be enforced upon successors in title provided they satisfy defined tests. Also available is Section 111 of the Local Government Act 1972 which can be used to allow a local authority to receive money or assets to discharge its functions.

DOE Circular 22/83 (Welsh Office 46/83), sets out guidance for dealing with planning gain (obligations or benefits which extend beyond the development for which planning permission has been sought). This is based upon the Property Advisory Group report of October 1981, which followed a series of charges that LPAs had 'sold' planning permissions in return for public benefits (e.g. retail permission in return for a swimming pool). As with all circulars it is purely advisory, and since planning gain is cemented by an agreement between consenting parties, and there is no possibility of referral to the Secretary of State, the circular has even less weight than normal. The recourse for a developer who feels that too much is being asked is to refuse to sign the agreement. If a planning refusal results, the LPA will have to defend its decision on planning grounds – and may well be embarrassed by public revelations of attempts to secure benefits beyond the terms of the circular. Costs may well be awarded in such cases. Alternatively, an agreement which is outside the scope of the relevant section of the Act of Parliament could be challenged in the courts – a point of which LPAs need to be aware since they cannot then withdraw the permission!

In the circular, the term planning gain is defined much more narrowly than in common usage. The definition excludes any terms or conditions involved in the disposal of land by a local authority, as well as matters arising from other legislation, such as requisitioning the provision of a water supply or of a public sewer. The most common usage is to require from a developer provision of (or contribution to) a public facility, the need for which stems from the development. Frequent examples are a contribution of public open space, a donation for public parking, or the provision of a community facility related to the development. The use of conditions cannot secure these benefits. The normal process is that the legal agreement is conditional upon planning consent, and is signed before the planning consent is granted. A local planning authority cannot undertake to issue a planning permission as part of an agreement: this would be to 'fetter' its future decision, which it cannot legally do.

Conversely, a developer may well feel that his willingness to enter into an agreement to provide a (relevant) planning gain will strengthen his case in the event of an appeal. Equally the LPA may well wish to ensure that should it lose the appeal, the gain will still be forthcoming. Hence the value of a conditional agreement previously negotiated and signed. This can save considerable time later.

Planning gain is a negotiated process and therefore presumes willing parties on either side. The ground rules proposed by the circular are:

1. Planning gain should only arise where it stems from 'proper' planning considerations: the provisions of the development plan and any other material considerations. Planning gain should not be used by the

developer to 'buy' an unacceptable planning consent, nor should a planning application be used by the LPA to demand extraneous benefit.

2. The obligation must be reasonable, by which is meant that either it must be necessary to enable the development to go ahead (e.g. adequate access, sewerage facility): in the case of financial payments to secure the facility, this should be within a reasonable period of time; or development would not be permitted without it (e.g. car park or open space) or it would secure an acceptable balance of uses in a mixed scheme.

3. The *extent* of the obligation must be reasonable in relation to the scale of the development, e.g. a retail scheme might be used to gain local road improvements, but not miles of dual carriageway; and it should be a reasonable charge on the developer (as distinct from what ought to be publicly funded).

There are various points of which the developer should be aware. Firstly, some gifts can turn out to be liabilities! To offer land or capital provision or a facility to a local authority may seem to be providing a benefit but the local authority has to consider whether it has the revenue budget available to maintain open space, say, or to run a swimming pool. It has also to avoid receiving shells and being unable to fit them out. If future operation is intended to lie in the private or voluntary sectors, then the local authority has to be sure that such a facility will be commercially viable or attract reliable community support.

Secondly, it is important for developers to pre-plan the process of negotiation: they should not offer planning gain too early as it may not be required if the development is attractive to the LPA on other counts. Clearly there is a direct relationship between the cost of planning gain and the overall relationship between costs and values in the development appraisal. The developer cannot, for example, expect to be bailed out by grants like City Grant: DOE appraisers are briefed to ensure public grant does not pay for planning gain. Local authorities may, however, choose to 'top up' a total package that offers clear benefits to the community at a lower price than direct provision.

Thirdly, there are the mechanics of the agreement. The legal niceties of how planning gain is cemented sometimes do not stand too close examination. For example, there may be a resolution of the LPA that planning permission will be forthcoming in the event of the legal agreement confirming the gain being signed. But legally the LPA is not bound by such resolutions, only by the specific grant of planning permission. As explained earlier, it cannot limit its future jurisdiction by putting constraints on the process of determining a planning application.

All this reinforces the need for careful groundwork and reconnaissance on the part of the developer, and for a good *total* relationship between developer and LPA.

Partnership with the Local Authority as Landowner

The relationship between a local authority as landowner and as planning authority has always been difficult. Local authorities are empowered (Town and Country Planning General Regulations 1976) to grant permissions on land they own, for development by others. Although the various Acts give local authorities wide discretion to undertake land deals, they are required at the same time, by the Local Government Act 1972, to obtain the best possible price within valid planning assumptions for land they sell, unless they get the specific consent of the Secretary of State to do otherwise. Thus, there is clear scope for manipulating the planning process to benefit council-owned land. At the same time the temptation is also there, not least because the issue of betterment arising from planning permissions has never been properly tackled (although various efforts have been made to regulate it and the related question of compensation).

Compensation remains an essential part of the system, for example in compulsory purchase legislation. Betterment (i.e. the return to the community of some of the value in land that the community, as opposed to the developer, has created) has always been a harder concept, and all attempts systematically to define or measure betterment have failed – the most recent being the Community Land Act. Absence of a codified system of betterment is one of the main justifications for planning gain; it can also prompt local authorities to buy land before publication of planning proposals, as another way (alongside planning gain) of returning value to the community.

Use of land ownership in this way can have extremely beneficial results: the classic instance is the development of Edinburgh New Town (the area that includes Princes Street) in the late eighteenth century. The city council bought land to the north of the Old Town, which was at that time separated from the area by a deep depression (the North Loch) filled mainly with sewage. Having done this, the council filled in the Loch (now Princes Street Gardens) and built a causeway across it. The increased land values fully recouped the outlay (indeed, paid for many public facilities), and permitted the imposition of extremely stringent covenants on the form of (private) development of the New Town. It is ironic that recent restrictions on 'barter' deals (in the 1988 Finance Act) may have made such an approach more difficult now than it was then.

Edinburgh New Town is a good example of sound estate management and planning working together (and many more recent examples could be given, not least the post-war new towns), but there are also cases of the reverse: longer term planning aims being compromised for short-term profit on land. The aim of successful developments in successful places requires the combined efforts of public and private partners to avoid such short-sighted expediencies.

Some of these general points on the interaction of planning, planning gain and land ownership can be illustrated by a case study. This will be followed through the various stages from initial brief to completion of the development with a commentary on the issues and techniques at each stage. It opens at the point where the council has decided it needs a partner.

A Case Study of Commercial Civic Development of a Central Site

The site 1980   The central area site is partly occupied by the first phase of a civic development: later phases have been delayed by resource problems. The site is generally in a poor state, despite some cosmetic treatment.

The proposal   After some years the council has concluded that it is unlikely to have the resources to complete its development and has decided to seek a developer for a joint scheme in order to complete the site. The development brief is for:

civic accommodation to complete parts of the original scheme, for which the local
    authority is to pay;
commercial development to be undertaken by the developer on the remaining
    land, which will be sold. The council wants a hotel as part of this scheme;
a multi-storey car park to be constructed on an adjoining site to serve the
    development, because of access restrictions to the site itself;
an overall design brief relating to the scale and character of the development.

Possible Approaches to Disposal of Local Authority Land

There is a wide range of techniques available by which a local authority can sell land or select developers:

Selection of developer   Formal tender; informal tender; expressions of interest followed by interview; straight allocation.

Disposal practice   Freehold, leasehold (premium or share of rack rent), equity stake.

Method of control (if any)   Building agreement, development brief, development agreement.

These numerous possibilities do suggest that, from the outset, prospective developers need to establish what the local authority's objectives are and to have a thorough understanding of the process involved, the terms of disposal and the method of control over the development, if any.

Ownership of land offers the local authority a greater opportunity to mould the form of development, and if the form is important to it, it has the ability to secure it, using land ownership powers, which exceed planning powers in certainty of enforcement.

The LPA can compulsorily purchase land to assist a private development, but there are a number of caveats: (a) procedures are lengthy; (b) there is a lack of certainty − objectors have a right to a public local inquiry, and there would need to be a sound public policy rationale to be reasonably sure of success. Generally, only the largest and most complex schemes are likely to justify the time, risk and expense of seeking compulsory purchase if the local authority does not already own the land. Moreover, the developers will have to give an open-ended indemnity on costs and demonstrate that they alone can realise the scheme.

Case Study: Part 2

> *The process*   Developers are invited to submit schemes and financial offers for development of the site in terms of the brief. Elected members select the best bid (on a combination of offer and content) after advice from the officers and a presentation by the developers' teams.
>
> Months pass and selected developer concedes he cannot proceed. Second choice is approached.

Local Authority As Brokers/Financial Enablers

In the days of Urban Development Grants, local authorities were able to supplement their range of inducements to developers by sponsoring UDG schemes for submission to DOE. Several used section 52 agreements to *pay out* the grant (a reversal of the original objectives of that piece of legislation, but still perfectly legal!). Since May 1988 local authorities continue to have a role in sponsoring and encouraging proposals for City Grant (successor of UDG), but not directly in its appraisal, execution or payment which is wholly in the hands of DOE. Nevertheless, pro-active authorities will still be able to promote desirable developments, though whether with the same ability, local motivation and relationships is not yet certain.

Inherent in this form of grant-aid is the relationship between grant and land value since the development appraisal calculation automatically raises the grant if the land value increases. It is entirely right that the prospect or achievement of grant should not stimulate artificially high land values. On the other hand, when local authorities are disposing of land to developers who apply for a grant they must ensure that the price paid by the developer is not artificially low, unless it is with consent of the Secretary of State.

Case Study: Part 3

After discussion with the new developers' team, a UDG submission is made by the council to DOE. The basis of the submission is UDG support for the hotel, car park (to serve the whole development), and for refurbishment of the existing shopping parade link. Commercial (office) development and civic works to be financed without assistance, but included within an integrated scheme. Long negotiations involving DOE appraisal team, city council officers, the developer and hotel operators bring eventual success. UDG of about one third of the total cost for the hotel, and £1m towards the multi-storey car park is agreed. The civic works and shopping parade refurbishment is to proceed with direct council funding; offices to proceed on private sector funding without grant (total development value: around ten times UDG).

Joint Schemes

At simplest, a local authority can dispose of its land in return for a share of the rack rent, thereby achieving a joint development with a developer/ funder. That will normally be a straightforward negotiation. Over the last ten years, though, local authorities have increasingly turned to forming joint companies, or wholly owned companies, in order to unshackle themselves from the limitations on local authority freedom of action. For the developer negotiating with such companies it is important to recognise that the company exists for specific reasons and objectives, the scope of which could be much narrower than that of the parent authority, although the company will have greater freedom to act commercially within that scope. Such differences will impinge upon the nature and process of negotiations.

APPENDIX 1   SUBMITTING A PLANNING APPLICATION

Submission of Application

The better the application, the easier it will be to handle. Developers should pay attention to the pre-submission advice from the planners and from their guidance notes, and to these points:

They should deal correctly with the ownership certificates which form part of the application form.

Applications for certain forms of development need advertising by the applicant prior to submission (e.g. buildings in excess of 15m high, buildings for indoor games). If the applicant cuts corners here he will waste time.

They should define the application properly, making clear the nature and extent of permission required.

If the application is complicated or high profile the applicant should send in more copies than requested.

They should consider consulting adjoining occupiers themselves as the council will consult them. A better reaction may be gained from neighbours if they are approached at an early stage.

Local Authority Consultation

There are a number of forms of consultation and participation in planning decisions – some are statutory, some are discretionary. Consultation on developments will be dealt with in some of the following ways.

Statutory public consultation   Where LPAs are obliged to advertise or to consult with amenity societies such as the Victorian Society, and the Georgian Society, and to announce certain defined forms of development in newspapers and on site.

Statutory consultation with public bodies in defined cases   Where applications are referred for comment to such bodies as county councils, water authorities, Department of Transport, and the Health and Safety Executive.

Consultation within the council   Where other departments have to deal with issues such as highways, environmental pollution and landscaping.

Consultation with residents adjoining the site   Although consultation with local councillors, residents' associations and individuals is discretionary, there are approved ground rules to observe, determined by the authority.

Formulation of Officer's Report/Recommendation

This is the vital part of the process. A wide range of issues are drawn together in order to reach a considered view:

local feelings about the development
relevant approved plans and policies of the council
other departmental or government body views
government advice from circulars
the planning officer's understanding of the committee's objectives, which will be
    influenced by its decisions on previous applications.

Committee Decision and Document

Only on very rare occasions are applicants afforded the opportunity to address the committee. It is likely that the developer can attend − but not speak. The decision document will then arrive or can be collected by the applicant. It needs careful examination because it is a legal document. The developer should check the conditions to see that they relate to his understanding of the negotiation.

APPENDIX 2   LEGAL ASPECTS OF PLANNING GAIN*

CONDITIONS ON PLANNING PERMISSION

1. The scope for using conditional planning permissions under Part III of the Town and Country Planning Act 1971 for the purpose of imposing positive obligations on developers is subject to limitations described in Ministry of Housing and Local Government and Welsh Office Circulars 5/68 (currently being revised). Any conditions must achieve a proper planning purpose, be relevant to the development authorised by the permission and be reasonable in other respects.
2. Some local planning authorities have, under local Acts of Parliament, powers to impose conditions which are additional to those mentioned in this Annex or to enter into other forms of agreement.

SCOPE FOR AGREEMENTS:

SECTION 52 OF THE TOWN AND COUNTRY PLANNING ACT 1971

3. Local authorities are given express powers under section 52 of the Town and Country Planning Act 1971 to enter into Agreements with persons having an interest in land for the purpose of 'restricting or regulating the development or use of the land'. The advantage of using section 52 is that provisions in such agreements which are in the nature of negative covenants are, by virtue of sub-section (2) enforceable by the local planning authority against successors in title of the person or body who entered into the agreement. Positive covenants can be included in such agreements provided that they achieve the purpose of restricting or regulating the use or development of the land. Incidental and consequential provisions (including provisions of a financial character) which are considered necessary or expedient for the purposes of the agreement may also be included. It should be noted that a developer cannot be required to enter into such an agreement by means of a planning condition.

SECTION 111 OF THE LOCAL GOVERNMENT ACT 1972

4. There is a general power for local authorities to make agreements with developers in section 111 of the Local Government Act 1972. It gives local authorities power 'to do anything (whether or not involving the expenditure, borrowing or lending of money or the acquisition or disposal of any property or rights) which is calculated to facilitate, or is conducive or incidental to, the

discharge of their functions'. The section would, for instance enable agreements to be made for the payment of money or the transfer of assets to a local authority where this will facilitate the discharge of the functions of the authority. The section does not empower the local authority to require such a transfer; the transfer must be by agreement.

POSITIVE OBLIGATIONS RUNNING WITH THE LAND

5. Some kinds of positive obligations or covenants can be enforced against successors in title by virtue of section 33 of the Local Government (Miscellaneous Provisions) Act 1982 which has replaced section 126 of the Housing Act 1974. These are covenants which are entered into by a person with an interest in land undertaking to carry out works or to do any other thing on or in relation to that land; and they must be contained in an agreement (made under seal) which:

(a) is made for the purpose of securing the carrying out of works on land in the Council's area in which the person entering into the covenant has an interest; or

(b) is made for the purpose of facilitating the development of land (in or outside the Council's area) in which he has an interest; or

(c) is made for the purpose of regulating the use of land (in or outside the Council's area) in which he has an interest (e.g. an agreement to use some of the land as a car park to serve the development on the remainder); or

(d) is otherwise connected with land in which the person entering into the covenant has an interest (e.g. an obligation to carry out certain demolition or other works or to pay towards the cost of such works if carried out by the Council).

AGREEMENTS UNDER THE HIGHWAYS ACT 1980

6. In certain circumstances, a highway authority who are proposing to carry out works can enter into an agreement with a developer under section 278 of the Highways Act 1980 to carry out the works in a particular manner or to begin or complete the works by a particular date for the benefit of the developer in return for the making of a contribution by the developer towards the cost of the works.

*Reproduced from Department of the Environment Circular 22/83, Planning Gain, 25 August 1983.

APPENDIX 3   SELECT LIST OF GOVERNMENT CIRCULARS

The Department of the Environment's Index of Extant Circulars (January 1988) lists over 130 as still containing material of current relevance. In addition there are nine Development Control Policy Notes, and eleven of a new series of Planning Policy Guidance Notes. The following is a select list.

CIRCULARS
(DOE Reference Nos. and brief guide to contents)

Procedural

Development Plans

    22/84: Structure and local plans: procedures and contents
    24/87: Changes to local plan provisions
    25/87: Simplified planning zones

Development Control

    71/73: Publicity for planning applications/development proposals
    1/83: Rights of way – alteration/recording procedures
    1/85: Use of conditions on planning permissions
    3/86: 1985 changes to General Development Order
    2/87: Grounds for awards of costs of planning appeals

Land Valuation/Acquisition

    167/74: Planning basis for assessing compulsory purchase price
    13/83: Use of purchase notices
    6/85: Compulsory purchase order procedures
    15/85: Restrictions on compensation for planning refusals

Policy

General

    22/80: Advice to LPAs on relaxation of planning controls
    22/85: Guidance on 'planning gain'

Subject Guidance

14/84: Green belt: definition and policy on development in
15/84: Housing land, and land studies
16/84: Encouraging industrial development
14/85: Importance of employment resulting from development
28/85: Role of derelict land, and derelict land grant
2/86: Small businesses: need for LPA flexibility
21/86: Government policy on large shopping developments
8/87: Historic Buildings/Conservation Areas – policies and procedures

Site Factors

10/73: Noise – use of planning system to deal with problems
9/84: Planning control over/near hazardous developments
31/85: Aesthetic control – scope of planning system
16/87: Agricultural land – considerations affecting development

DEVELOPMENT CONTROL POLICY NOTES
(Being replaced by Planning Policy Guidance Notes)

DCPN2 (1969): Development in residential areas – infill, etc.
DCPN4 (1969): Development in rural areas – agricultural dwellings, re-use, etc.
DCPN5 (1969): Development in town centres – comprehensive development, parking, traffic, conservation
DCPN6 (1969): Road safety – development affecting highways
DCPN8 (1969): Caravan sites – planning/site licensing
DCPN9 (1969): Petrol filling stations/motels – siting
DCPN11 (1969): Service uses in shopping areas – planning considerations
DCPN12 (1972): Hotels and motels – planning considerations
DCPN16 (1985): Access for the disabled – planning considerations

PLANNING POLICY GUIDANCE NOTES (1988)
(These are superseding DCPNs. and *may* supersede the 'policy' circulars that they summarise. Circulars would then be reserved for advice on procedures and legislation – see Circular 1/88)

PPG1: General policy and principles
PPG2: Green belts
PPG3: Land for housing
PPG4: Industrial and commercial development and small firms
PPG5: Simplified planning zones
PPG6: Major retail development

PPG7: Rural enterprise and development
PPG8: Telecommunications
PPG9: Regional guidance for the south east

There are also two notes on Minerals Planning Guidance:

MPG1: General considerations/the development plan system
MPG2: Applications, permissions and conditions

THE PLANNING APPLICATION PROCESS

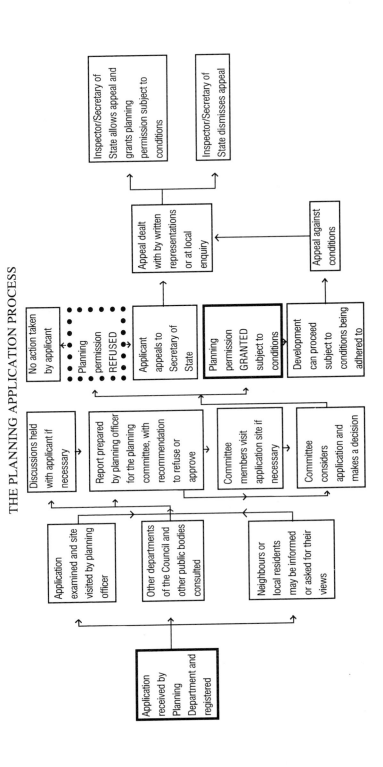

INDEX

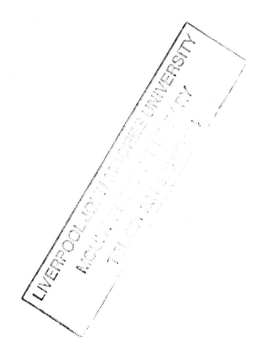